The Essential Kenneth Leslie

The Essential Kenneth Leslie

selected by Zachariah Wells

The Porcupine's Quill

Library and Archives Canada Cataloguing in Publication

Leslie, Kenneth, 1892–1974
The essential Kenneth Leslie / selected by Zachariah Wells.

(Essential poets; 5)
ISBN 978-0-88984-328-8

I. Wells, Zachariah, 1976– II. Title.
III. Series: Essential poets (Erin, Ont.); 5

PS8523.E77A6 2010 C811'.52 C2009-906355-7

1 2 3 4 • 13 12 11 10

Grateful acknowledgment is made to Rosaleen Leslie Dickson, the daughter of Kenneth Leslie, for permission to reproduce the poems in this volume.

Published by The Porcupine's Quill, 68 Main Street, PO Box 160, Erin, Ontario N0B 1T0. http://porcupinesquill.ca

Represented in Canada by the Literary Press Group.
Trade orders are available from University of Toronto Press.

We acknowledge the support of the Ontario Arts Council and the Canada Council for the Arts for our publishing program. The financial support of the Government of Canada through the Book Publishing Industry Development Program is also gratefully acknowledged. Thanks, also, to the Government of Ontario through the Ontario Media Development Corporation's Ontario Book Initiative.

Canada

ONTARIO ARTS COUNCIL
CONSEIL DES ARTS DE L'ONTARIO

Canada Council for the Arts
Conseil des Arts du Canada

Contents

Foreword

I first encountered a Kenneth Leslie poem in the anthology *In Fine Form*, published in 2005. Humbly titled 'Sonnet' there, it was (I later learned) the untitled fifth poem from the title sequence of *By Stubborn Stars*, Leslie's Governor General's Award-winning 1938 collection. Further trawls through anthologies suggested to me that Kate Braid and Sandy Shreve, the editors of *In Fine Form*, must have found this poem in Margaret Atwood's Oxford UP anthology of Canadian poetry. While hunting for content for my own forthcoming compilation of Canadian sonnets, I found the poem again in, of all places, John Fuller's *Oxford Book of Sonnets*.

For all its formal perfection and emotional resonance, the stubborn endurance of this poem also signals a significant loss. The poem stands alone beautifully, but what the most recent anthologizations of it fail to announce is that it is only 1/28th of one of the best long poems ever published in Canada. I don't dispute that this is the finest sonnet in 'By Stubborn Stars', nor indeed that it is the best short poem ever published by Leslie – but there are several pieces in the series nearly as good, as A.J.M Smith maintained in the introduction to one of his anthologies, and the suite itself cannot be excerpted without doing damage to it, and to our sense of Leslie's most important poetic accomplishment.

One explanation for Leslie's all-but-disappearance is his old-fashionedness. Leslie, whom Milton Acorn called 'the loveliest of our orthodox sonneteers', was keenly aware that the verse he wrote was out of step with Modernism and the exhortation of Pound – seven years Leslie's senior – to 'make it new': 'I cannot sing a new song, / I fear to sing the old' is how he begins a poem that ends with Pound's very phrase. If the chart for Leslie's poetic course was doubtful – to modify the opening line of the title sonnet of 'By Stubborn Stars' – it didn't keep him from proceeding headlong: 'I sail by stubborn stars, let rocks take heed, / and should I sink ... then sinking be my creed!'

That closing couplet tosses a mooring line of sense and rhyme to a poet who died by drowning over a century earlier. Shelley, born almost exactly a hundred years before Leslie, wrote in his own sonnet sequence, 'I fall upon the thorns of life! I bleed!' There are striking parallels, biographical and poetic, between Leslie and Shelley. Both were resolutely unconventional iconoclasts, idealists, radicals; both founded anti-establishment magazines (Shelley, *The Liberal*; Leslie, *The Protestant*) – though Leslie lived to see his through several years' worth of issues before it foundered – both believed in, and worked for, changes to the legislation of the world, and both ran afoul of political authorities for their trouble.

Leslie hated dichotomies, hated the world's insistence that we make a choice. If faced with Frost's fork in the road, he would opt to travel both ways at once. Although he cleaved to inherited British, Romantic modes of poetic speech – perhaps because he did so, stubbornly ignoring the fashions of modernism and later of Olsonian Projective Verse – Leslie believed in a Whitmanesque embrace of contradiction, the fusion of apparent antinomies.

So many things in Leslie cut both ways; in the sixth sonnet of 'By Stubborn Stars', 'Green ebbs away' signifies the recession of life and vitality while in the ninth, it is death itself that is green. As Burris Devanney says, 'the ambiguity of Leslie's political message persists and seems to allow for no final synthesis. He is indeed throughout his poetry remarkably consistent in this one inconsistency.' This can and should be extended to all aspects of his life and works, not just to his politics. Easier to gather up an armload of live herring than to fix Leslie in any synthetic scheme.

Leslie hated everything that engenders dullness and conformity. In 'Tea with the Professor', a satirical sonnet with a carpe diem theme, the speaker urges the Professor to 'Hang history and its seven thousand years', to let himself be engulfed by 'this "now", that, narrowed to a name / for what is not, was never, nor can be', and ends 'Your ifs and ands, your wisdom, heavy and old, / walk on my heart ... your tea is getting cold!'

He develops this theme at greater length in 'Cobweb College'. The freshman class at the College 'are ghosts of boys, cracked wide with knowledge, / their dreams dried out and left the dreamers dead', already bereft of 'illusion' and 'romance', no vital force left in them for the College's Spider to suck out, he having 'drawn their blood too many generations/and spoiled the breed'. In a memorable simile, Doctor Spider describes their wills as being '"like the blown pigskin that drools / November muck around a soggy field." All they want are the Professor's "ifs, ...ands, ...buts."'

It's not hard to imagine what Leslie would think of today's Creative Writing industry, snugly ensconced in the folds of academe, star pupils destined to become tomorrow's teachers, poets acting more as bureaucrats than as legislators, safe in a hermetic world of their own. In such a climate of diminished expectations for poets and poetry, it makes sense that Leslie's peculiar brand of ambitious but non-careerist poetic excellence, his fusion of the radical and the traditional, of the personal and the public, of the wild and the sophisticated, of musical grace and raw emotion, should have sunk almost out of sight. Although Leslie loved romance and illusion, he anticipated his future obscurity with clairvoyant sangfroid in 'Street Cry,' the coda to 'By Stubborn Stars'. But he also prophesied those readers 'in some uncut page of time' who have kept, and who will continue to keep, his words alive.

– ZACHARIAH WELLS

Open Lading

I have a barge of dreams, have I,
but never a town to tow it to.
        I'll let it go on the waters that flow.

I have a seed of grass, have I,
but never a field to sow it to.
        I'll let it fly on the air that goes by.

I have a sheaf of words, have I,
but never a soul to show it to.
        I'll let it roam … it will find a home.

New Song

I cannot sing a new song,
  I fear to sing the old,
and I would sing a love song
  to melt a heart of gold.

Should my note fall where the old note falls
  I surely would be blamed;
yet for their ancient madrigals
  thrushes are not ashamed,

and thirsty buttercups are filled
  with oft-repeated showers
and year on year the swale is thrilled
  with old familiar flowers.

So I must put the song above
  the tune I sing it to;
and if you listen kindly, love,
  your tears will make it new.

By Stubborn Stars

Dedication

Some day when you grow up you will discover
the reason you and I must stay apart –
my madcap dancer, my haphazard lover –
will find it in your own too ready heart,
impetuous feet, too eager lips and eyes,
that ever look and ever headlong run
to touch the face of beauty, will be wise
too late and sprawl your length, as I have done.
I think I hear you now. The gathering gray
lifts from my mind this instant to a sweet
and shrill inconsequence; the inspired play
of histrionic fancy, the frenzied beat
of your original hornpipe makes me glad
I had you, son, the little time I had.

*

Once as I watched the clear air of your eyes
the shadow of a wildly beating wing
touched the horizon of our candid skies
and broke their brightness with sharp winnowing;
passion was swift upon us, sweeping us clean
into the strait beyond the harbour wall;
the hooded hurricane curled, the raging green
swallowed the light, swallowed the bell's call.
And yet, not even when the reef had swung,
slow and implacable, its iron gate
out, out against us till we heard its tongue
clicking the cruel knowledge of our fate,
would I believe its stupid blinding lies,
remembering the clear air of your eyes.

There is no secret from the misty mother
mumbling old ballads to the stones that creep
down where Atlantis and many a lost other
slip from earth's memory to her sunless keep.
Tales that were stirring the bright air are stilled
forever in the black silt of her floor;
her caves are choked, her crevasses are filled
with tales of love and after-tales of war.
There is no mountain-top but must come home
to taste the salt against her heaving side,
no crag but is an exiled reef whose foam
flashes a far white longing for her tide.
And with our happy tears and tears of woe
we too shall swell her song with what we know.

*

It would be heaven to happen by a room
and see you both, my well beloved, there,
whom I have loved against the face of doom,
each finding in the other something fair,
as once before, finding that lovely thing
that I behold now shining from both of you,
clear impulse of these wounded words that sing
of tender gray eyes as of brooding blue.
Just to walk by and see you resting there
filling the casual time with quiet talk
of intimate things; it is too much to dare
to hope for, and I know the wind must mock
my wish; but even so I wish some day
you could be taking tea in the old way.

The silver herring throbbed thick in my seine,
silver of life, life's silver sheen of glory;
my hands, cut with the cold, hurt with the pain
of hauling the net, pulled the heavy dory,
heavy with life, low in the water, deep
plunged to the gunwale's lips in the stress of rowing,
the pulse of rowing that puts the world to sleep,
world within world endlessly ebbing, flowing.
At length you stood on the landing and you cried,
with quick low cries you timed me stroke on stroke
as I steadily won my way with the fulling tide
and crossed the threshold where the last wave broke
and coasted over the step of water and threw
straight through the air my mooring line to you.

*

The cold resistance of your lips was here
upon my lips, and on my hand your hand
dropped down and trembled in a frost of fear;
your eyes were wet and red with reprimand
against the sharp decree of circumstance
we had allowed to rob us of our right.
You would not speak, but plainly in your glance
I read the truth and knew my shameful plight.
Green ebbs away, the garden is a dust
gathering grayness on a coloured cape,
the stars are futile perforations thrust
into the night by one who would escape
this crotched necessity of standing true
to her while pledging life and love to you.

The day reeled downward from a heavy blow,
the golden day that raced upon the moor.
I saw her there; I missed seeing her go;
my face was bright with her, she seemed so sure,
when the black spruce dragged her beneath the skirt
of the low hill; I would hardly believe
she could be quite away; but there was the hurt
under the side of my heart, and my torn sleeve.
What must I do, now I see she is gone,
as the bit of blue sleeve is gone too?
Each hour of the dark my pain finds its dawn,
and nothing is deeper mine than the missing blue.
What must I do now, what curse can I say
against the coming treason of new day?

*

The waters of my life, lying so still,
dreaming a stagnant dream of coming light
that never came, now stir and suddenly spill
between high narrowing banks that clasp them tight,
closer and closer clasp them till they run,
in anger first with froth and ferment blowing
for freedom lost, then little by little won
into the silent business of swift going.
Strong, I am strong, and yet no more resist
your spirit that is channeled deep to mine;
For courage in your quiet lips has kissed
my lips to courage as with solemn wine.
Now, though I have no choice, I choose to go
and find you where your salt tides ebb and flow.

The chart is doubtful for the course I take,
and even without the chart I sense green death
and choking weeds that bind a lost keepsake
with that poor thing, love-inside-out, whose breath
is love's last cry. Why then am I so dour
and dogged in my sailing, deaf to the din
of tongues that are quite sure, oh bitter sure
honour is lost and all else loss to win?
I only know the canvas of my soul
is crying out against these narrow places,
is fain for unwalled water and the roll
of smoky seas and fog-fermented spaces.
I sail by stubborn stars, let rocks take heed,
and should I sink ... then sinking be my creed!

*

Seldom are words as empty as that king's
who taught his vassals how what was to be
must come to be in the deep tide of things,
teaching with waves beside the northern sea.
Words were the prize for ancient deeds of glory
dared by heroes dreaming all the time
how they would swell the ballad singer's story
and live forever meshed in magic rhyme.
Life has its flower in words, and only so
blow down upon us from the olden days
those far-borne fragrances by which we know
there was a yesterday, whose potent ways
crowd in our consciences till we forget
that yesterday is in the making yet.

This soul was sick and found in my soul kin
of the same sickness, for my similar ill
spoke in the wordless language of that sin;
the flaws fit perfectly beyond our will.
As any broken limb, if set in vain
and wrongly set, though fresh and firmly grown,
must be re-broken and re-set in pain,
so does the broken spirit seek its own.
Through matched incompetence we can forgive
each in the other what you could not bide;
the fool that flinches death yet fears to live,
the brave that haunts the field yet runs to hide.
Your scorn has cleared my path; then take no heed;
strength to your strength be joined, need to my need.

*

'Twas finer stabbing this, stabbing to life,
and sweeter vengeance, spinning out the death;
'twas canny cruelty to stay the knife
that would have snuffed out memory with breath.
Not that I plead against the hissing thrust
of white-hot anger tempered to a point
of austere law that finds with savouring lust,
knowing it well, my vulnerable joint.
But who am I to speak of such a plight
to her, for did not I do ill to one
I desperately loved, for which a night
of black unreason blotted out her sun
and she did back to me a deeper ill,
so that we hurt each other past our will?

A steady breath has blown the veiling sedge
out of my vision. In that breath I see
the wide Atlantic and this monster ledge
of granite under granite clouds; these three,
the solid sky, the water ramming the shore,
thrusting its hills of green against the hills
of grim set pride, and their engendering war
from which life and my thought of life distils.
A strange distillage, while the sad airs wail
the witless actors on their drafty stage,
heedless of hearers, mouthing their foaming tale
of bitter feud no hammering can assuage,
that I, salt-spawned, should choke upon a tide
of iron pity, wearing down my pride.

*

Sometimes when turning a page I toss the book
aside and wonder what book you are reading,
and sometimes walking along a road I look
far off and wonder what way yours is leading.
I seem to see you in a crowd and race
all out of breath to catch you before you go
quite out of sight; then we are face to face,
and you are polite and listen to my 'hello!'
You look straight into my eyes and shake your head
as if to recall a once familiar name;
you say, 'But don't you know that you are dead?'
and I am confused and clasp my coat with shame
and go back to my book, but there the word
has lost its meaning and the print is blurred.

Your tears fell frozen; numbing the heart your tears
fell on that final night of our reprieve;
across the threshold idiot-visaged fears
crowded your mind and made your mind believe
my heart was sealed behind a stolid wall,
so twenty years of life took wings to fly
and beat their sad way through the empty hall,
and twenty years of love lay down to die.
Not you alone were stricken by the sword
flashed in our quick 'good-bye', not you alone
were shaken when its sharp and quivering chord
shattered our world. And though the overtone
follows me where I walk and will not die,
that death my steps declare, I still deny.

*

My love is sleeping; but her body seems
awake within itself, secure from ills
of consciousness; her veins are buried streams,
her flanks are ghostly vales, her breasts are hills
of some far planet finding its sure way
beyond the orbit of this night of fears,
beyond the burnished darkness of this day;
my love is sleeping out of reach of tears.
How can her limbs dance motionless, what makes
her lips curve smiling to a crescent moon,
what does her hand reach out for, what dawn breaks
beneath her eyelids, to her ears what tune?
I shall not sleep, nor seek that yonder land
where her hand yearns, but not to touch my hand.

Pause for Query

Why do you good folk stare so hard at me?
Of what are you afraid? that I may take
a breath of air as if the air were free?
that I may eat and sleep and dare to wake?
and feel the sun you feel? and walk abroad
upon the warm earth whose wet grasses flow
to quench your feet, not mine? What sort of God
gave you the key to bind or loose me so?
Is it because within my self you've seen
your dark selves branching like an evil tree,
and with my growth your illness thickens green,
that you forever grind your axe for me?
Then finish grinding, lay it to the root
of your ill thinking, lest your thought bear fruit!

*

A hand unburied on a battlefield
might well express my features who remain
alive upon the earth, nor yet quite yield
to dissolution, tell how I disdain
the pity of kind friends for this distress,
nor ask the pity of my God whose grace
is a drawn sword, but I must learn to bless,
if only dust, then dust in my embrace.
Let me forget what carried me away,
let me forget the body that I served,
let me be lying open while the day
slowly runs out between my fingers curved,
keeping no thing at all in my control,
saving no thing except perhaps my soul.

This is a casual love then, so you say,
coming and going as the light that weaves
a wavering pattern on a windy day
upon the pathway through the moving leaves,
sifting itself in such an easy fashion
that we are caught with it before we know,
holding it in our burning-glass of passion,
and hate its coming, knowing it must go.
As if the giver or given could control
the myriad laws and counter-laws of need,
as if a calculation in the soul
could parcel heaven's hunger from hell's greed!
So, it is cold and casual, you say.
Cold as the sun! Casual as the day!

*

Have I then pressed white iron on your eyes,
and have I seized your proffered hands and flung
their kindness down, and did I wreak surprise
against your spoken candour? Did my tongue
launch sudden horrors on your frightened ears?
Then I have thrust myself beyond the edge
of your forgiveness, and these tardy tears
smarten my penance for the sacrilege.
Dear love, your love is both a life and death
in me, its whetted point is buried deep
and double-barbed against my barest breath,
so that I want no waking, dare no sleep.
Know then, my breath, my sleeping, and my waking,
that I am breaking too when you are breaking.

A warm rain whispers, but the earth knows best
and turns a deaf ear, waiting for the snow,
the foam of bloom forgotten, the rolling crest
of green forgotten and the fruit swelling slow.
The shearing plough was here and cut the mould
and shouldered over the heavy rain-soaked lands,
letting the hot breath out for the quiet cold
to reach deep down with comfort in its hands.
The sap is ebbing from the tips of the trees
to the dry and secret heart, hiding away
from the blade still green with stubborn memories;
down in the roots it closes the door of clay
on grief and growing and this late warm rain
babbling false promises in the pasture lane.

*

The Valley streams lie open to the tide
and to the second light that, now the sun
is hid, pours headier wine into the wide
meadow that stretches beneath Blomidon.
Look, then, and draw your fill of liquid light,
dreaming with me upon this drowning shore
that we are one forever and no night
can drive a wedge between us any more.
Drain the bright Basin ere that sombre barque,
freighted with dusk behind the Ardoise Hills,
casts her black shadow on the last flood-mark;
drink hard against the night while heaven spills,
and shut your ears upon that sound of weeping
there in the shadow where the ebb goes creeping.

An old sharp cry comes back to me again,
to my heart through the break that your heart made,
a collie's cry herding the cows to the lane
from the meadow pasture. I had been afraid
it was forgotten, but the falling bars
are quickly near me and the stable's night,
hoofs stumbling to the stanchions and the stars
bathing the orchard with unshadowed light.
You have brought back the hurt in the heart's
core for a dog's death and the shrill swelling joy
of riding a load of hay through the barn door
and the sweet dizzying airs an earth-sick boy
breathed and still breathes on that clean farm,
breathes now and breathes forever, safe from harm.

*

I was put out of countenance by bloom,
as if a dark mind could be such a dark
that it would push away into a gloom
the glow of petals and would smudge the mark
of sun-gold on a face or book or rug,
as if a coward mind could unfold wings
and fly abreast of midnight, mad to hug
its blindness from the sharp lit edge of things.
But now that I am truly blind I frown
with inward vision on a wild parade
of colour rich and deep enough to drown
the outward eye, straining to hold one shade,
striving no more to push them from their place:
the rose, the rug, the sun-gold on a face.

Day slipped out of the web of her fog-wet gown
and buried her bright face in the pale sheen
of the maple leaves and pushed her fingers down
in the damp moss under the deeper green
of the darkling spruce and found a cool mind
and turned and looked back through the lucent panes
of maple leaves at the sky she had left behind
and traced each pointed leaf and its intricate veins.
Lying there she shook with a sudden mirth
and waited awhile without breathing a breath
and nestled closer into the hollow earth
and knew a bliss that would have welcomed death,
knowing she could not deeper drink delight,
and she dreamed there of shadow and of night.

*

There was no time to talk, manoeuvring through
those sharp-set seas, no time to take a breath,
beating between the teeth of gales that blew
us inch by inch upon a jagged death.
A hand could touch a hand, changing the wheel,
an eye could catch the quick glance of an eye,
clawing from hell with one sail and a keel
against the stark persuasion of the sky.
Now we have time to tell the worth of waking
through weary watches in the throat-black night,
tell it together with the dawn-wind shaking
new sails alive, proud wings of a bird in flight,
tell the tamed sky and the quiet blue,
the canvas filled with air, I filled with you.

Tempest is done, the winds of time are tame;
the world is air breathing out of the west;
the world is water whispering a name,
water to bow whispering rest, rest.
The wind is song, a quiet song in the shrouds;
the world is home, home is the wide world;
the sails are piled up white to the white clouds,
the sails are filled and no sail is furled.
In creaming light, in crested joy they climb
beyond the skysails where a homely sound
is cradled out of the roving winds of time
that move with mystery from the blue profound.
Stand with me here on the smooth deck until
the song has healed our wounds and soothed our ill.

*

Street Cry

I build my stand here in the market-place
and show my wares, but no one stops to buy;
and so my purse is empty, and my face
screws hunger's yawn into the smiling lie
that all is well. Yet beating in my rhyme
persists a prophecy, a confidence
that three souls in some uncut page of time
may find my book and say, 'Here is the sense
of our necessity ... "never quite wrong
the heart's request however less than wise!"
Happy those ancient ones to hear his song!
Surely this singer looked through honest eyes!'
Against a cold wind, thinking of my heirs,
therefore, I hammer away and shout my wares.

Success

There was a dream;
he fulfilled it.
There was a wish;
it came true.
There was a fire;
and he killed it.
There was a spark;
and it flew!

The Preacher

To Albert Cohoe

Constrained to call and cry the wares of God,
you stumble in the pulpit, troubled, dumb,
suddenly stricken, silent as a clod,
no whispered word, not even a breath will come.
What strange antagonist takes strangle hold
upon your spirit's tendons till they bend
to breaking, and yet leaves your spirit bold
to claim a victor's blessing at the end?
There! He has gone, and going swings a gate
for swift release. Your throat, a golden flume,
the flowing torrent of a soul in spate,
mad with *hwyl* of spirit, fills the room.
Now we can guess the pain, the silent cry,
and whose hand struck the hollow of your thigh.

Halibut Cove Harvest

The kettle sang the boy to a half-sleep;
and the stir, stir of the kettle's lid
drummed a new age
into the boy's day-dream.
His mind strove with the mind of steam
and conquered it
and pressed it down and shaped it
to the panting giant
whose breath lies heavy on the world.

This is a song of harvest;
the weather thickens with a harsh wind
on this salt-seared coast;
offshore a trawler, smoke-smearing the horizon,
reaps the sea.

Here on the beach
in the cove of the handliner
rain flattens the ungathered dulse,
and no cheek reddens to the rain.
From the knock-kneed landing
a faltering path is lost among the rocks
to a door that is closed with a nail.
Seams widen and the paint falls off in curling flakes
from the brave, the bold so little time ago,
the dory high and dry,
anchored in hungry grass.

This is the song of harvest:
the belching trawler raping the sea,
the cobweb ghosts against the window
watching the wilderness uproot the doorsill with a weed.

The Hill Heart

Easing my pack with the pull of the sky,
I climbed the great hill and won
to an old clearing, full of the ghosts
of a hill-farm abandoned.
I asked them, the broken churn,
the rotted step, the roofless ruin,
the grindstone drowned in grass, I asked them
and their living comrades, brown-top and lilac,
to escape what harm this homesteader
had flown from the fertile valley
to plough and plant and churn butter
up here half out of the world.

... the lilac answered, leaning
from the dooryard over the sorrow
of the sunken cellar ...
No harm at all, it was just a farmer
got claustrophobia in the valley.
From here it was not the hill was far,
'twas the valley was far. The center
was here on the hill. When the young'ns moved back
to the valley
the heart lost hold of the hill.

The Word Had Need of Flesh

Though my soul without control
die beneath its yoke of dust,
yet the word had need of flesh;
so there's reason in my lust.

Aestheticize, anaesthetize,
one is mist, the other fog.
Propriety, licentiousness,
two names, but the same old dog!

The good soil is corrupted,
and deadly clean the snow.
Pull the root of the wormy fruit
and where will the fine fruit grow?

Cobweb College

An Antinomian Parable written for Robert Frost

A batch of freshmen came to Cobweb College;
the Spider looked them over, frowned and said,
'These boys are ghosts of boys, cracked wide with knowledge,
their dreams dried out and left the dreamers dead.
There's not a meal among them, no illusion
to sharpen up my tooth on, no romance
for me to ridicule to red confusion,
no creed on which to slake my poison lance.
I've drawn their blood too many generations
and spoiled the breed. Their fathers, when I wrapped them
in causal web and silken strong equations,
would lunge and writhe, grimacing when I snapped them
with categoried claws. These modern schools
condition them until they yearn to yield;
their wills are like the blown pigskin that drools
November muck around a soggy field.
They murmur, "Say, Professor, skip the prodding,
just dish it out, the ifs, the ands, the buts!
who'd question fifty million miles of wadding
engendered through the ages in your guts?
Welcome the warm cocoon of cosy thought
through which we gain the world but lose surprise!
we'll answer by your book, old man, but not
pretend amazement,"
                                        thus the pampered flies
and those who hope for pampering … the rest
nursing a schoolboy grudge within the core
of mangy-bearded justice are at best
a thin and scanty ration for my store.'

So modernly at his wits' end to find
food for his pattern-maw: as when old cries
were battle banners for the foolish blind;
or wisdom knelt before the prattling Wise;

or doddering knights clanked forth as to a feast
and opened old wounds for an empty tomb
while on their heads the stupefying East
poured her unholy oil to their sure doom;
or as when that rough shepherd whose wild head
ached noisily pulled from the pasture mire
her heavy brogues and herded kings instead
and burned two kingdoms in her fagots' fire;
or as when hare-brained Shelley turned the tack,
unwigged the judge, lifted the felon bard
out of his cage onto the judge's sack
and placed the moral guardian under guard;
('twas Shelley solved it) he would find a poet
and pen him just beyond the edge of knowledge
(tether him well but never let him know it)
to be a milch-fly for old Cobweb College.

'Come, then, quaint poet, feed them hints of God
my hounds of two-plus-two-are-four will chew!
Cast over them your old divining rod
and draw their deep springs to my sultry view!'
Thus came the Ageless One to Cobweb College
and said,
'It is incumbent upon me
to be the thing that I was dreamed to be;
the word I say and live will not divide;
it must be born complete.'
His voice cross-grained,
he said it sitting on a class-room table,
not lotus-seated but legs swinging free,
a very Yankee Buddha (if a Buddha),
leaving it once to look abstractedly
out of the open window at the sky,
smiling to welcome in the coming storm,
the quick low murmur and the sudden dark,
his voice the thunder's texture and his hands
its muscled wind, veined lightning. The storm broke.
'Lately we hear much talk about selection.

I'll dip some random uses of that word
out of the pot where words boil up in deeds:
"What is your selection for the Derby?"
"The new headmaster is a good selection."
"Out of these evils I select the least."
"The most important thing you learn at college
is how to live your life selectively,
to recognize the seal of excellence,
the caste-mark of those persons one should know,
the hallmark of those books that one should read."
Easy to note the part selection plays;
yet here's the antiphon, the song's recoil:
(what we forget is that it works two ways)
the seed is chosen by and chooses soil.
Not difficult to choose things ready made
and marked with price-tags, plainly stamped and signed
or guaranteed by cliques and claques of critics;
but making things is more than choosing things.
It is the hardened artery of the soul
that delves in *objets d'art*, jostling the good
and bad of artists' and no-artists' leavings
conducted by a melancholy dealer
who wears upon his one and only eye
a disc of gold and rubs his hands to hear
the dry voice of a dowager exclaim:

> "What a pretty crucifix,
> Only seventeen and six!
> Just the thing I want to fill
> that bit of wall-space ... what a thrill!"

Here is a simple parable of life:
The bark upon a tree is wood; it peels
year after year while holding to its form,
its form tradition, and its peeling off
the yielding of tradition to the sap
of new creation ... so we have the tree.
Now teach the bark its business with steel bands

and twist those bands until they choke the sap …
steel bands for the pharisee, for him
no living tree but stark unbending branches
on which to nail the Life that loves through death …
steel bands for the graceless scholar; he
tallies three kinds of grace, A, B and C,
snuffing the living flame with adjectives
saying "How quaint, how quite Wordsworthian!"
The slowed-up poetry of speculation,
the Martha role of keeping things in order,
the retail merchant sorting and arranging
the world's goods on his hierarchic shelves …
there is a deeper thing on which these bud,
a passion that is too much in the blood,
too moving in the marrow of the loin,
too much the chosen itself to mould a coin
whose metal face would blind the human face
and shut it from the inner holy place.
Rather than moulds invisible in the air
into which petals pour selective milk
I seem to sense a partnered agony
of creature and creator in the rose,
and in each act of mine there dwells a host
of that same pair, a host with the strange power
of swinging wide the door for them to enter
or slamming it against me, I that host.'

There was a frantic scurrying in their minds,
a rush to find appropriate pigeon holes
for all this tangle; nothing seemed to fit.
The Spider sidled in with a quick squeak
and a suggestion born of sudden fear
that rather than a lecture once a week
a better plan would be one once a year.
The Ageless One heard (not the interjection)
the scurrying to and fro within their minds:
yet he went on in that most sublime faith
that ever life goes seeking for its own

leaving the indexed husks ... here in this very room
might brood a boy with hunger strong enough
to smell the truth. Now there began to sprout
in Doctor Spider's brain a horrible doubt ...
What gender was this animal? What ilk?
Gin for his tender babes if this was milk!

'The hundredth sheep was not a select sheep,
but just a sheep that happened to be lost.
Mary would have loved her Son as much
had he been but the unrepentent thief.
Do lovers tally points of excellence
as if they were self-breeding animals?
(I speak of breeding; it involves selection.)
You may breed long legs thus, even long heads,
but love is neither bred nor educated.
Love knows no grammar, yet the stiffest lock,
the dullest door, may open to his knock.
Tradition, once as subtle as the film
that wraps unfelt the living nerve and vein,
begins to choke the vein and lull the nerve
to liking it; the film is wire now
and coalesces to a band of steel
so that a good professor is a blacksmith
or combination smith and spi – ...'
                                                                The Spider
dwindled with a squeak until his gown
seemed hung in mid-air on a wire hanger,
his mortar sagged upon a shrunken peg.
The storm had passed beyond the folded hills,
only its curious echo in this room,
this man's rough voice its far threat of thunder.
'From soil somehow the poet's word
and from that word the spreading tree
where swells all fruit, sings every bird,
whose strong trunk is philosophy,
whose branches thrust in legal maze,
whose leaves are myriad windows green

sifting the one to many ways,
tinting the unseen to the seen.
Your teachers list the birds and fruit,
the trunk and branches of the tree;
but they forget about the root,
because the root they cannot see.
Yet have the roots a ray to find
their road between the stones and clay;
like Raftery,* the singing blind,
better than day they know the day!'

Tea with the Professor

Hang history and its seven thousand years,
be merciful, this moment bends its knee!
You rave of Marlborough's hopes, of Caesar's fears,
while I pour heaven out of a pot of tea.
Tomorrow knows but what today will tell
in night's confessional, 'now' stays to mock
not long enough to ring its passing bell,
not long enough to mark it on the clock;
and yet this 'now', that, narrowed to a name
for what is not, was never, nor can be,
holds in its crystal cup the liquid flame,
eternal brew of world and you and me.
Your ifs and ands, your wisdom, heavy and old,
walk on my heart ... your tea is getting cold!

Harlem Preacher

To Martin Luther King

The gospel song, hushed suddenly to a hum,
dies in vibrating silence; a child clings
to its mother, wondering what is to come.
The preacher closes his eyes and waits till wings
have winnowed the world of guile, then lifts his head
with flash of power and grace no art can teach,
now softly repeats the text that he had read,
and, throwing himself away, begins to preach.
Not arguments but God Himself, the Maker,
worlds for His whims, the Dreamer and the Doer,
the Lover, cruel and kind, the Heart-breaker,
wayward and jealous, the mad and mighty Wooer,
God in the flesh is what this black man brings,
into the hungry throng it is himself he flings.

The Candy Maker

To James Moir

Somebody asked me this the other day:
who are the pure and passionate of heart?
I said I had known one, long years ago,
a gaunt and gray man, not a poor man either,
a 'business man' of the old pre-war kind
who'd built his business slowly on its worth,
or, rather, let his worth build up his business.
He was a manufacturer, a candy maker.
He knew what other men had learned of sugar,
its idiosyncrasies from cane to crystal,
and went beyond them, like a pioneer,
knowing no boundaries in his passionate quest
of knowledge that was pure and diamond-sharp
to etch in definite form his venturing taste.
I used to love to watch his inward mind
rove, as he slowly chewed a grain of cacao,
to Java, Venezuela, or Ceylon,
tasting at once its source, appraising it.
He had a special gentle way to draw
the easily hurt soul of the vanilla,
to tempt the curious waywardness of creams,
to make a caramel that would be true
to the 'dear honey' that is in its name.
His feet were on the ground, his head was high,
he walked in nature's straight and narrow road.
I never knew that purity was passion
until I saw this gaunt and gray-beard man.

Windward Rock

To James Moir

White, tooth-marked by the gray sea wolves, you face
their fury, break their fangs against your side,
letting them slither from your hard embrace
to whine their death-cry on the ebbing tide.
You guard my cove and lure the minted moon
within its peace-bound flood, you save my fishing,
you let my kettle and my cradle croon,
friending my field to harvest past all wishing.
Two faces so you keep, one for those others,
grim, unrelenting, one turned from the sea,
sharing the scanty hope of earth-born brothers
that somehow all things are as they should be.
There blows my blessing on an outward air,
a wild-rose petal for your granite hair!

It Cannot Be Easy

To Robert Norwood

It cannot be easy now any more
to watch the day go from the Cove
when the flaming weeds along the shore
deepen the dark of the softwood grove,

not easy to sing when the singer is gone,
to love when the lover has slipped away,
to hold the heat of the sun that shone
in a summer that died in its longest day.

The man with the pipe and the sailor's song
went out for a walk and he walked too far,
wherever he went he has stayed too long …
The light on the foam is a burned-out star.

Sorrow Must Sing

The tale of sorrow is not reckoned well
in anchored words; it must upsail and go
with thick voiced winds upon the rhythmic swell
of deep sea music and each word must know
more than it knew before; the dismal hold
of this weed destined barque may hint yet hide
the utter hopelessness that would be told,
so in the telling some strange hope may bide.
Yes in the telling, in the setting forth
there shall be snow white sails and rainbow gleams
upon prow-broken waters, the lost north
must shine at least within our willful dreams
for sorrow is a living learning thing
and breaks our hearts which broken hearts must sing.

To My Father Drowned at Sea

They said that days would doctor my great ill,
would grow as good as new what grief had set;
and so I waited while they worked their will;
but twenty slow years had availed not yet
to end the long drouth nor to quench the pain
that scorched away the green blades of my sowing,
sending but fickle gusts of teasing rain
to sprout for withering what might be growing.
This day the dry road has a phosphor gleam,
the grassland flows to water for your child,
your salty laughter breaks my sullen dream
and all the world runs wet and deep and wild.
You stood your trick on deck through my long sleeping,
hands on the wheel, eyes to the weather keeping!

Lowlands Low

What can be better than to let the screen of years
fold up and leave a boy,
a fireplace and a man there singing?
The last light dying from the coals, the last note dying
in the ears of the song-captured idolater ...
remembering days that shall not be again
except this way, remembering,
letting the image enter well-used doors,
the smell of Harris tweed and English leather,
the smell of 'Old Chum' smoking,
the clean aroma of a man.
No words to hint the quality of his voice,
the salt-edge in it, the sweet and vibrant sorrow.

No way to hint the quality of his eyes,
set bold and challenging, yet queerly shy,
dark mirrors of a boy's unslaked delight
in all things various and strange,
in all the heaped-up helping life had served him.

His song, The Lowlands Low, not mouthed from a book
but taken alive and terrible from the sea ...
to remember the thickening in my throat
when 'his shipmates picked him up and on the deck he died',
the brave boy, the betrayal, the irreparable loss,
my father's eyes half-closed upon the last long note,
'and they sank him in the Lowlands Low!'

The screen of years unfolds again
and pushes this strange semblance of myself
into this strange semblance of my city.
He, too, is gone the way of the sea
and is lost in the Lowlands Low ...
and I am left here with no token, no watch or knife or book,
by which to call him back,
but I remember here in my throat his song,
remembering.

Beauty Is Something You Can Weigh in Scales

Beauty is something you can weigh in scales
and wrap up into parcels, it is known
not well in dreams, in evanescent tales
of misted rapture, of bugles faintly blown.
'Tis meat as well as music, from the ground
it grows up in a tree, stands in a wall.
The earth belongs to beauty, it is earth-bound,
seen, heard, smelled, tasted, or not known at all.
I found it first and best in father's store,
measuring yards of calico, weighing out nails,
sprawled among nets and cod-lines on the floor,
venturing cut-brier, rifling candy-pails.
Beauty was my mother's porridge in a bowl.
Milk, oatmeal, and molasses built my soul.

Cape Breton Lullaby

Driftwood is burning blue,
  wild walk the wall shadows,
night winds go riding by,
  go riding by the Lochie meadows.
On to the ring of day
  flows Myra's stream, singing,
Cadil gu lo, laddie, sleep the stars away!

Far on Ben Breea's side
  wander the lost lambies
here, there, and everywhere,
  and everywhere their troubled mammies
find them and fold them deep,
  fold them to sleep singing,
Cadil gu lo, laddie, lo, laddie, sleep the moon away!

Daddie is on the Bay;
  he'll keep the pot brewin'
keep all from tumblin' down,
  from tumblin' down to wrack and ruin.
Pray Mary send him home,
  Safe from the foam, singing,
Cadil gu lo, laddie, lo, laddie, sleep the dark away!

Rory's Praise of Elspeth

For D.J. MacDougal

In Barra Glen I found my bright woman; her hair is a flame.
She is my wife through the church and a treasure;
she is my pulse and my joy and my pleasure … and torment,
she is my love, and quick to boil over like milk on the hearthstone,
and the touch of her hand is the law and the prophets.

Last Saturday dawn I was pulled by a salmon
off the black rock at Myra,
but I gathered the prize from the mouth of misfortune
and took the bright boyo ashore in my arms.

In the Gulch all that day I was telling the tale
and drowning with Phil of the Bottle the taste of brown water.
The story was staling when I ventured homeward, light foot
        and light heart,
a song in my soul and the salmon on shoulder for peace.

And peace well enough I walked into …
I could sniff her afar like the wind off the ice-fields;
I could see her arise like the spread of a scowl in the sky over Smoky.
Caressing a thole pin she rose up to greet me.
Then the darkness came down and it stayed till the dawn,
when I rose with a storm in my head.
Oh she is my love and my joy
and her hand is the law and the prophets!

Jesus Thought Long

Jesus thought long
    on an oar thinned to breaking.
It was flesh in His hands
    of hard toil partaking.
Jesus found beauty
    in the curl of a shaving
And truth in a yoke
    worn out and past saving.

Guide

On the meed
of His Yea
I feed.
On the rock
of his Nay
I walk.

The Old Man

In an old-fashioned village in the Lunenburg hills
I met a little old man who carried a gnarled stick
and whose brown cheeks had thin red veins
like golden russet apples and whose eyes
were clear and fathomless like mountain pools.
By the side of the road was a pile of fallen leaves
where children loved to romp with their bare legs
as children do in these far-away old-fashioned places;
and the wee man moved his stick gently through the leaves.

'Listen,' he said, 'they are whispering,
and this is what they are whispering:
"Our time in the bright air was fulfilled,
and without complaint we wrapped ourselves in our richest garments.
Without a word we let go and launched out
upon our first and last journey,
flashing a glad good-bye to the world of wind and stars.
We have not fallen.
We have come up out of the sky to this earth-star,
to clothe the ground with glamour and to whisper
strange wild things to the bare feet of boys and girls.
For they, too, must say good-bye.
Their time must be fulfilled.
Not long before the boy will be but a memory in the heart
of the man as the leaves
will be but a memory in the heart of the tree."'

Tasseled Thought

I've walked about since birth;
wet, when I stoop to eat
the tasseled wheat
I put roots in the earth,
and, finding there my home,
coolly I burn
and greenly like a fern,
my feet in the soft loam.
It is then disesteem
to make pretence I am not
a tasseled thought,
a smouldering leafy dream.

Early Summer Storm

To Eileen Curran

Shaken, torn,
by my yearly getting born,
waiting while my Mother weaves
leaves,

clothing me
as she clothes each naked tree,
and giving me, instead of singing birds,
words,

fiercely warm
comes an early summer storm,
twists from all my wintry length
strength.

Requiescam

I must have peace, must have it undisturbed,
quiet and deep, must have it in my soul,
deep in my soul. But let no noise be curbed,
let every restless thing escape control
and find its freedom in its own sweet groove!
Let eagles storm the sky, let the worm creep,
let all things move the way that they must move,
but let me rest awhile and let me sleep!
And do not chide me for my weary eyes,
nor scold because my hands have lost their grip.
Some arrows they have aimed still climb the skies,
some hands shall not forget their comradeship.
I must have sleep and leave the quickened clay
to answer if sleep bring another day!

Lir's Daughter

To Andrew Merkel

A moody princess rides within the path
of royal waters crested with rich foam,
puts throat behind the laughter and the wrath
of wild and wooing wind, tempers the dome
of hurrying cloud and cold unhurried star;
she is more cruel than the jutting granite
thrust from the sea's floor, and lonelier far,
more lost and broken than the screaming gannet.
Your heart has heard the challenge of her cry,
your tiller hand that senses flaw and tide
has trembled on her, and your shameless eye
has darkened when she laid her robe aside.

The Computer

It is the buried old that spawns the new,
it is finality that spreads the feast
and sets cold teeth behind warm lips to chew
the killed thing, be it fruit or bird or beast.

Habit is death to impulse and a song
is shamed whose singing grows habitual.
Yet men must eat and men must carry along
their heritage in custom and in ritual.

And this machine, this habit chilled to steel,
this stealthy anaesthesia of the hand,
this row of rigid numbers that can feel
no shade of yielding in their stark command,
yes, even with this our will may weave a cage
wherein protected we may sing our rage!

Last Sleep

You sit before the fire and nod
and gather up within your brain
your 'thousand nights' of joy and pain
to lay them in the lap of God.

Your book of days slips to the floor,
the ink is faded and a word
unfinished on the page is blurred;
you do not write there any more.

The trembling fingers of the day
falter, reluctant, at your chair,
and from your brow and from your hair
take light and shadow both away.

No Poem Is Ever Ended

You cannot say a poem is ever ended
or catalogued once for all;
in each new age and in each new eye
the word will swell and dwindle,
the grain of dust will be the cornerstone,
the cornerstone will be blown away like ashes in a storm.
The childish rhyme will become a home-thrust
deep to eternal truth,
and the resonant high-piled line will be a witless music,
an empty and pretentious tune.
Ever each poem must be tried on by new pilgrims,
and, as it fits, fulfills new destiny;
for spirit speaks to spirit
as a child's heart in a secret forest, dark,
beats out quick answer
to the spruce cone
suddenly falling
from the aged spruce.

About Kenneth Leslie

Leslie was born on Hallowe'en night, 1892, in Pictou, Nova Scotia, to Robert Jamieson Leslie, a politician and businessman, and Bertie (Starratt) Leslie. Robert Leslie died on December 4, 1905, when one of his own boats, the steamship *Lunenburg*, sank in a storm off the Magdalen Islands, the jurisdiction he represented in the Quebec legislature. The younger Leslie would memorialize his father in his sonnet 'To My Father Drowned at Sea' and in the free verse dirge 'Lowlands Low'.

Leslie was educated at Dalhousie, Nebraska and Harvard, where he would have received a Ph.D. in Philosophy, had he not failed the lingual test. He had a deeply ambivalent relationship with institutional education; he revered the best of his teachers and worked as one himself on several occasions, but distrusted universities, which he saw as breeding grounds for dullness and conformity, as is manifest in his satirical sonnet 'Tea with the Professor' and especially in his long satire 'Cobweb College'.

Most of Leslie's career as a publishing poet was confined to the mid-to-late 1930s, a probable cause for his slide into obscurity. His first book, *Windward Rock*, was published by MacMillan in 1934, followed quickly by *Lowlands Low* in 1935 and *Such a Din!* in 1936, both of which were privately published. In 1938, Ryerson published *By Stubborn Stars*, which won the Governor General's Award. He would not publish another book until 1971, when The Ladysmith Press released *The Poems of Kenneth Leslie*. Angered by editor Sean Haldane's exclusion of several poems 'because they seem not to have worn as well with the passage of time, or because they were light verse, or political verse, which fulfilled a temporal need', Leslie self-published the unexpurgated *O'Malley to the Reds and Other Poems* in 1972.

For Leslie, as for his contemporary F.R. Scott, politics were at least as important as poetry. Living in New York and Boston in the 1930s and '40s, Leslie rose to prominence as an indefatigable anti-Fascist activist. Somewhat paradoxically, Leslie's socialism was inextricably intertwined with his Baptist upbringing. He founded and edited *The Protestant Digest* (later renamed *The Protestant*), which reached a circulation of 50,000 at its peak, and he was much in demand as a speaker. He also started *The Challenger,* an anti-Fascist comic book that appeared in 1944 and '45. For his troubles, Leslie was named – along with such notables as Arthur Miller, Albert Einstein, Aaron Copland, Leonard Bernstein, Norman Mailer, Charlie Chaplin, Thomas Mann and Langston Hughes – as one of fifty 'dupes and fellow-travelers' of Communism by *Life* magazine in 1949.

Leslie's personal life was no less tumultuous than his public affairs. His first wife was Elizabeth Moir, daughter of wealthy chocolate-maker James Moir. James Moir made a considerable impression on his son-in-law, who dedicated two poems to him. The breakup of Leslie's marriage – and his consequent estrangement from his children – is the subject of 'By Stubborn Stars'. His second marriage, to Marjorie Finlay Hewitt, ended because of an affair Leslie had with his secretary, Cathy, with whom he returned to Halifax in 1949, where Leslie took up work as a taxi driver. The much younger woman would leave her husband for his nephew. In 1960, Leslie married the widow of an old friend, Nora Steenerson Totten, with whom he lived until his death on 7 October, 1974.

Since his passing, little notice has been paid to Leslie and his work, but recent anthologizations of his poems, as well as a documentary film, *God's Red Poet,* are signs that Leslie won't easily be forgotten.

About Zachariah Wells

Zachariah Wells was born in 1976 in Charlottetown and raised in Hazel Grove, Prince Edward Island. At the age of fifteen he left home to attend high school in Ottawa and has since lived in many parts of Canada (Halifax, Iqaluit, Montreal, Resolute Bay and Vancouver), working as a freelance writer/editor and in various occupations in the transportation sector. Wells received an International Baccalaureate Diploma from Ashbury College and a BA in English from Dalhousie University/University of King's College in 1999. He first started writing poems seriously in 1998. His poems, reviews and essays have been published and anthologized widely. He is the author of three chapbooks: *Fool's Errand* (Saturday Morning Chapbooks, 2004), *Ludicrous Parole* (Mercutio Press, 2005) and *After the Blizzard* (Littlefishcart Press, 2008). Also published are two trade poetry collections – *Unsettled* (Insomniac Press, 2004) and *Track & Trace* (Biblioasis, 2009) – as well as a children's story, *Anything But Hank!* (Biblioasis, 2008). He is also the editor of the anthology *Jailbreaks: 99 Canadian Sonnets* (Biblioasis, 2008). With his wife and son, he lives in Halifax, the only city he likes well enough to have moved to three times, where he works seasonally for Via Rail Canada as an onboard attendant and edits reviews for *Canadian Notes & Queries* magazine.